FORREST OLDHAM

Honey Run
Tribute

ISBN: Softcover   978-1-9845-7015-4
       Hardcover   978-1-9845-7016-1
       EBook   978-1-9845-7014-7

Print information available on the last page

Rev. date: 12/20/2018

To order additional copies of this book, contact:
Xlibris
1-888-795-4274
www.Xlibris.com
Orders@Xlibris.com

Contents

DEDICATIONS

Most dedications are for people in the author's life that encouraged, inspired, or otherwise helped the author to get the task of the book writing done. I choose a different tack for this space given the situation. I am having difficulty as I write this and work through the words due to the many emotions running in my mind from sad to glad.

It is a collection of horrible and compassionate events that come together to want me to list those that follow.

I would like to dedicate this book to firstly, all first responders, Fire, Ambulance, Law enforcement, OES,etc. Secondly, The comforters of the affected, such as those that run the food kitchens, the shelter volunteer helpers, and such. Thirdly, the follow up people that help those unfortunate to rebuild their lives.

Most importantly I very much dedicate this book to those displaced, and those passed as a function of the unfortunate series of events written of here.

In addition, though of much less importance to immediate events, I would like to dedicate to those that share(d) in the care and use of the Honey Run Covered Bridge.

PREFACE

What have I done? In my first published book "California Covered Bridges Pre 1900's" I stated in the preface that I asked myself "What can I do with all this?" meaning all my photos and information collected about California's Covered Bridges. Very shortly before the book was available California experienced, as of this writing, it's most deadly and destructive wildfire. Along with the tens of thousands of people displaced, more than 70 dead, and thousands of houses and/or businesses turned to little more than heaps of charcoal, there occurred another tragic loss. One of the precious covered bridges written about burned to the ground and creek below it leaving only the end footings and four red support columns. Following pages describe the reasons for its value and the tragedy of the loss. Put simply, I cried, as I am starting to now, knowing the impact it had on many, many lives over its lifetime. I wanted to help people put their lives back together following the effects of the fire. Ideally I would see the bridge rebuilt, as well. To that end I questioned a good many people how best I could do this, including Xlibris, the publisher of the first book. It was suggested I write a tribute book to the bridge. They would expedite the printing. The proceeds then go to help the victims of the fire. My mind ran with the idea. Let's collect photos from other photo acquaintances that have photographed it over the years and put those photos with the photographer's comments in. Also needed would be photos of the bridges destruction to fully show the story. Add another twist, I am a rideshare driver that loves to chat with my passengers. The fire being the very biggest event around, I discovered not only the extent of the impact of the fire, but many who knew of the bridge and the events tied to the past. I collected some of these to share that you the reader may get a feeling for these impacts. Other material would add to the story which follows

Back to the opening question. I find myself on a deadline that cuts into my time enormously. The process is also an emotional roller coaster. All this I gladly do to help in my small way the poor victims of the fire known by the road it started on, Camp Road. What follows I hope the reader takes in and has greater understanding the impact on the lives of people our historical artifacts have. In addition, it is my hope lessons from the greater tragedy of the Camp Wildfire be learned well and applied to the future to best prevent any such similar event, if possible. While I touch a little on the fire itself, I leave that stories' telling to others with greater time, resources, and talent for doing so. Over the years of photographing the Covered Bridges of California, of which there are more than 80, I developed a fondness for them, their history, and the effect on their community. I am only the teller of this story from my perspective. In the end it is about the people, the bridge only being a focus I use to tell a small part of the story of the people

HISTORY OF HONEY RUN COVERED BRIDGE

California's Covered Bridges are a direct function of the 49er Gold Rush and the establishment of California as a state in the U. S. in 1850. Early on most roadway/trails followed the waterways with the terrain dictating the best path often needing to change the side to travel on. The bridges were built, with State Permission, by private people to allow for passage of commerce over waterways. Honey Run, built in 1890, spans Butte Creek which runs through a canyon north of what is now the Skyway Expressway. The Bridges were generally built by Eastern U. S. bridge builders the bridge of choice usually a covered bridge. The main structure usually using very large wooden members, longer spans in a truss, were covered with a lighter structure supporting inexpensive sacrificial coverings. This allowed the more expensive support members to last very long times with the coverings, usually of the least expensive nearby materials, to be replaced as necessary. Honey Run was unusual in that its middle roof section was higher than the ends. This construction served the Honey Run bridge well for over a century, in which it suffered through at least one other fire, thanks to firefighter effort saving it. Much more can be said for the construction over the years.

Honey Run, it is said, received its name when a couple was walking nearby that disturbed a bee's nest. One said to the other, "Run, Honey, run!" and they ran across the bridge. True or not, the name sticks. Through the years, as with many other bridges, it served people their transportation needs, as well as a focal point for weddings, other events, or general meeting place. It also served as the take-out point for Butte Creek float trippers. This bridge due to its relatively close location to larger cities and populations may have served these needs more than most other bridges.

As is the case for many of these historical icons Honey Run has a group of people dedicated to its cares and preservation. They were instrumental in saving it following the earlier fire in which a decision was made to replace it with a more modern bridge upstream. It remains to be seen what decisions will be made given all that stands due to the Camp Road Wildfire are the end footings, four red support columns, and a dedication plaque.

Plaque for Honey Run Covered Bridge. Photo by Rod Bradford.

DECISIONS OF PHOTOGRAPHERS

As photographers we make many decisions in creating our photos. Lighting, angles, and composition are common terms many know. In controlled smaller environments such as photo studios, lighting and other details can be changed as needed. Larger subjects, however, like structures and landscapes, dictate other ways of attending details to "get the best shot(s) possible. Lighting is dictated by time of day/year, weather, angle, reflectors, strong flashes, and or scheduling ability. Sometimes multiple visits may be necessary to satisfy the photographer's vision. Other factors are sensitivity to the situation such as photographing people and/or their events. Were you invited to do so, or are you "intruding"? Should you get in close, or stay out to share the environment? Each photographer brings to the table their own experiences, inspirations, and insights. This is all evidenced in the photographs of the photographers invited to share their works. What follows is only an example of the effect this bridge had on a very broad community, as other information will hopefully point out later in this writing.

One regret I have in my decisions is wishing I had "intruded" a bit more when I arrived on a follow up visit to find wedding preparations being made. I could have had more photos to share the importance of the bridge to many in the beginnings of their lives together. This, though, presents yet another problem, permissions. Legal issues face all of us on a regular basis. To use photos of people commercially a photographer must secure a "release". Additionally, for an author to use other people's creations, such as quotes or photos, a release is necessary. Many such legal issues face many others in this story, to be mentioned later.

The photographers represented here gladly share their works and hope the reader enjoys them and learns a little about how valuable such photographic subjects are that they attract all manner of photographers, casual to pro.

Above I chose showing rocks. below, riffles for the foreground. Both Photos required I risk the camera by wading into the river over slippery rocks, perhaps slipping and going for a swim. Such risks each photographer measures for themselves.

FORREST OLDHAM

At this point, I feel I must express, if I have not already, this is not about me. It is about the bridge, its impact on others, and hopefully that it can help those impacted by the Camp Road Fire. That being stated, each photographer will photograph the same "portion" of the bridge in their own way, which I hope you the reader will note as you page through. Each will choose different ways "to tell the story" with photos much different than others. What follows is a small bunch from each of us that we all hope you the reader will enjoy and ponder.

Above, in a front view I wanted to include angles of the bridge. Susan Bovey chooses a closer shot. Below, a quarter angle with hints of the wedding. Sue Graue chose a different time of year.

Interior vertical photo facing north showing trusses and roof structure.

Rod Bradford chose south facing to include the author

Quartering shot from low angle wanting to show water under the bridge and lower structure.

SUSAN BOVEY

Susan Bovey, a quickly improving photographer, photo club leader, and Real Estate person kindly contributed a few photos from years past.

Above, Susan's name plate close-up and below her interior photo.

Susan Bovey shows a close up of the upper corner of the bridge with the canyon wall background.

© Susan Bovey

SUE GRAUE

I do not know Sue Graue well as she is a member of the Hub Photo Club a bit away from my local club the Woodland Camera Forum. Rod Bradford, living a distance north of me and a similar distance south west of Sue belongs to both photo clubs. He asked me to be a judge one month of the Hub Club member photos. About a year later I was asked to come by again for the same purpose. As timing does, it was after the burning down of the Honey Run Bridge. This afforded the opportunity to ask if any of the Hub's members had photos of the bridge to share in this book. Sue stepped up with a couple wonderful examples, shown here, that also show the effect of decisions photographers make in their creations.

Each of us photographers chose a quarter shot of the bridge the difference being the year, time of day, or season when the shot was snapped. Sue appears to have arrived in the late fall for this wonderful photo. The fall colors are well represented.

Sue's interior shot uses well the lines of the bridge to help us look deep into the length of the bridge.

ROD BRADFORD

Rod, a fellow member of Woodland Camera Forum, I also consider a good friend. He has accompanied myself and a good many other members on a large number of photo excursions. One such was to Honey Run when and where the photos on these pages were made.

For the photo above on the left Rod chose a quarter shot opposite the chosen side of the others of us. The photo on the right is similar to one I chose, tight and low to the right side.

Above is Rod's version of the right side quarter photo of Honey Run.

Below shows the interior version as made by Rod. I am the photographer shown.

HONEY RUN COVERED BRIDGE

This is the view floaters on Butte Creek would see at this most popular takeout. We also see the grey weathered wood on the east side often seen on other covered bridges in California.

FLOAT TRIP TAKEOUT

RIDESHARE DRIVER

A recent development due to the computer and the internet is called rideshare. I am a rideshare driver helping people get where they need to go safely. These "rides" are of varying lengths of time, distance, and locations. During these "rides" many conversations will occur, often based on current events. While performing these during the period of the destruction by the Camp Road Fire some passengers would relate stories of themselves or people they knew affected by the fire or perhaps an event connected to the Honey Run Covered Bridge. Wanting to help long term some of the people affected and/or the rebuilding of the bridge I communicated with the publisher of my shortly to be available book on California Covered Bridges about ways to do this. Suggested was this tribute to the Honey Run Bridge with the Royalties to be used to help. After some thought, what you are reading is the result. I felt the story of the fire, while very sad, would be really important. What follows are just a little of the thoughts and feelings shared I managed to collect. I am sure there are very many, given the immensity of the fire, many more stories. Other more connected and professionally immersed people will no doubt cover those. While obtaining permissions, for legal reasons, from the people sharing, I do not necessarily share full names or other descriptions, to protect their privacy. Likewise, not being a reporter and needing to verify the accuracy of these stories, I have not fact checked. Given the situation, I believe the tellers were sharing as honestly as they could. I share some quotes, but otherwise tell in my words, hoping the feelings come through, their sharing's. It is my hope this helps those that read this not affected to understand those that were. I also hope that those affected will find some element of comfort (I struggle for the right words) as they read.

Shortly following the news of the fire, how fast it was moving due to strong winds, and the extensive travels of the smoke, a young lady and her 8-year-old daughter traveled with me. Her daughter asked why it was so smokey. The fire was 70 miles or so away north of our travels in southern Sacramento. Discussion moved to why they were in my car. They were escaping potential hazard, leaving home and job in Oroville, a city near the fire, behind. They had been part of the evacuation by more than 100,000 of the possibility the Oroville Dam would fail a year earlier. The mom said, "First water, now fire…".

About a week after the beginning of the fire I traveled north to attempt access to the area to make photos of the now fallen bridge. Authorities would not allow. I had an appointment for dinner prior to judging photos for the Hub Camera Club in Marysville/Yuba City, about 30 miles south. This meant I needed to stay in the area a little south of the fire. I stopped for a snack in a quick stop style market. I started to overhear stories of people there about their experiences with the fire. Talking with one of them led to the plight of a father/son couple. Raymond and Joel escaped with a car full of the dad's paintings. The dad, long retired, taught art at a nearby college and the son creates videos. The video gear as well as any other belongings short of the saved paintings were all lost to the fire.

One of the benefits of rideshare driving is being able to turn on/off the application as needed as well as driving most anywhere. I chose to drive for awhile near my dinner appointment to use my time to benefit, not only to me, but those that needed my services. I picked up a very young couple about 30 miles south of the fire in Marysville. Talk moved to why I was in the area, to photograph the bridge for this book and judge photos. They had a very new baby in a car seat that I guessed was 3-4 months old. They related they were escaping the fire as they lived very near the Honey Run Bridge. The mom, Stephanie, then stated, "I took my pregnancy pictures on that bridge." I had to ask their permission to relate this story.

Ken, another passenger, simply stated, "Uncle lost home."

One of the other tasks us rideshare drivers find ourselves doing is returning important items left in our cars. One such was a wallet left late the night before Thanksgiving while shuttling people between Cameron Park, El Dorado Hills, and Folsom, some 80 miles south/south east of the burn area. The only information at hand was the driver license address and name showing a location just a little south of Marysville/Yuba City. Given the holiday and likely the person was not at home I decided to wait until the Sunday following to travel once again north to get the needed photos of the bridge and combine possibly dropping off the wallet. The owner's father greeted me and accepted the wallet. Conversation moved to my being so far away from home which led to telling me his cousin lost not only his home, but a business employing 13 others. Was told his cousin cried for 5 days over the thoughts…

While at the bridge making my photos a small number of others came and went. We talked. One couple looking at the devastation said they drove over the bridge in the early seventies while it was still considered safe to do so. The reason they could remember when was they had their children with them.

Still at the bridge, another photographing the event related the bridge was a pullout landmark for drifts down Butte Creek, as well as a favorite place to share some moments while imbibing.

During the drive over the Thanksgiving Weekend one of the three members I was transporting on a drive perhaps about 15 minutes long asked me to tell a story. I shared my task of writing this book. The female passenger sitting next to me expressed living near the bridge in nearby Chico while going to Chico State University. She then said she regretted not going to see the bridge, and really wanted to. I had an 8X10 photo collage of photos of the bridge I shared with her. For the remainder of the trip she cried sharing remembrances and regrets about her experiences of that time. I told her to keep the photo collage...

November 13, 2018

By inscribing comment(s) and signature(s) below I (we) permit XLibris and Forrest Oldham to use said information in a book titled "Honey Run Covered Bridge Tribute".

My grandparents recently lost their home in the 2018 California Camp Fire. They were lucky enough to be at their second home in Oroville the night the fire hit, otherwise they'd have likely perished in the fire. Their neighbors awoke that night to the sound of glass breaking as their windows burst from the fire. They barely made it out with their lives.

-Danie

Danie

Above is one of the permission forms used to collect stories. It stands on itself.

The last names have been removed for privacy.

AFTERMATH

The Camp Road Fire is truly one of the most devastating events the State of California has seen. Even as of this writing there are more than 200 missing in this fire. Tens of thousands are displaced, not only from their homes, but their jobs. Memories are lost as artifacts were destroyed. Many of the people that lived in the affected area as well as those much farther away had some interaction with the area and the Honey Run Bridge. The bridge is only one of the "things" lost. I cover a little of the fire here only to demonstrate the vast effect it had on a large group of people. I am not here to assign blame or responsibility. I also use vague references to various parties as for me what is important is to learn from the event through asking questions, we can hopefully answer, to help reduce risk of another such event. I use photos to help the reader understand what was going on. This is by no means a definitive writing on this matter.

A week following the start of the fire found me driving as far away as Tracy, about 120 miles away, through heavy smoke. Passengers from San Francisco told of the same for there. Here, a photo of downtown Sacramento shows the density of the smoke at that time with the State Capitol Building peeking out down the street. Sacramento is about 70 miles south of the event.

A closeup of the California State Capitol Building in Sacramento is not fog bound, as is often the case normally, it is smoke surrounded.

About a week after the start of the fire I traveled north to attempt to photograph the poor state of the bridge. I was not allowed into the area. On such trips you can often make other photos. In this case I show what is thought to be a possible cause of the fire, that being power lines such as those to the left on the steel towers. Again, only one such cause, as there is talk of someone(s) intently setting fire near the power lines, as well as other sources of ignition.

About two weeks following the beginning of the fire another trip to photograph the remains of the bridge had us traveling up the Honey Run Canyon. Here we saw the above situation which had me asking the following questions"

1). Why so much underbrush under the power lines?
2). Is this private property and the owner supposed to clear?
3). Is the power company supposed to clear?
4). Are there Federal/State regulations preventing the clearing?

These are only a few questions to answer about the situation which reminds us we should not be quick to assign blame. One person I talked to relayed a story about a hunter friend of his that owned a large amount of huntable property. The hunter set about clearing out some underbrush leaving much of the cover intact to not only reduce the impact of a fire, but allow movement by people and large animals, which it turns out Native Americans did many years ago, also. He was handed a very heavy fine for doing so by a regulatory agency! Such a situation may exist for the parties involved where the fire originated.

FUTURE

What stands as partial reminders of the Camp Road Fire are shown above, the concrete footings, and below, a temporarily caution tape draped proud plaque. In the future will the bridge be rebuilt? Will the towns be repopulated and return to their former robustness? Will lessons be learned about the event that will be implemented to reduce or eliminate similar tragedies? I truly hope…

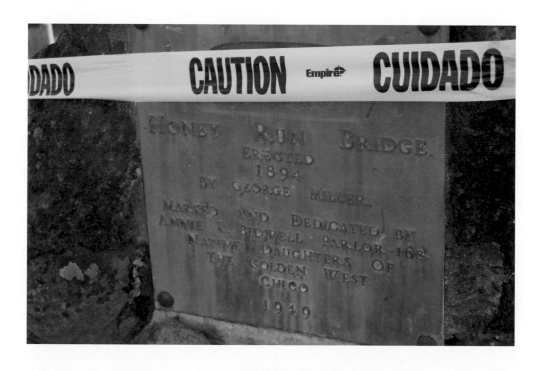

Printed in the United States
By Bookmasters

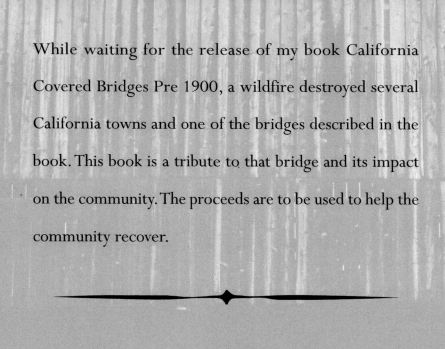

While waiting for the release of my book California Covered Bridges Pre 1900, a wildfire destroyed several California towns and one of the bridges described in the book. This book is a tribute to that bridge and its impact on the community. The proceeds are to be used to help the community recover.

With a limitless curiosity and some tools such as a full tank of gas, camera, fly rod, and computer, **Forrest** explores many places and experiences. He enjoys sharing with others to hopefully inspire others to "live their lives" by enriching experiences of their own choosing.

Xlibris

ISBN 978-1-9845-7015-4

52199

9 781984 570154

How Much Does
God Love Me?

Latonya Morgan